To:

From:

CHRISTMAS PRAYERS

by Marianne
Williamson

Illustrated by
Susan Zulauf

 PETER PAUPER PRESS, INC.
WHITE PLAINS, NEW YORK

Published by
Peter Pauper Press, Inc.
202 Mamaroneck Avenue
White Plains, NY 10601
All rights reserved
ISBN 978-0-88088-253-8
Printed in China
13 12 11 10 9 8

Visit us at www.peterpauper.com

TABLE OF
CONTENTS

I love Christmas
because it is a day when
many of us are more
emotionally honest with
those we love. "I just
called to say I love you"
is an authentic sentiment,
not just a song title, on
that particular day.

Life is sweeter, as millions of people throughout the world consider the possibility that a higher love exists. For one day we lay aside our cynicism—if not completely, then enough. We lay aside our faithlessness and our judgments and our blame.

We embrace the notion of
a light at the center of things
that casts out darkness and
casts out fear. Millions of
people think thoughts of love
on Christmas. That is why
it is an important day.
That is why it gives us joy.
That is why it is such a
blessing on the world.

M. W.

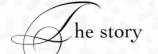The story
of Christmas began
with a visit from angels,
announcing that God's
love would be born
on earth.

It is the story
of the life of Jesus
two thousand years ago;
it is also the story
of a love that lives in
every one of us.

Each of us,
in a way, is visited
by angels every
time we have
a loving thought.
Angels are
the voices of faith

and peace and
forgiveness, sent
by God to illumine
our way. Let your voice
be heard and let your love
shine forth during this
magical time of the year.

✦ A PRAYER OF LOVE ✦

Dear God,
At this miraculous
moment,
may the light of Love
burst forth in my heart.
May Love's starlight
cast out all darkness
in my life.

May I become
the Love within me.
Help me speak with Love,
and act with Love,
and hear with Love,
and live with Love.

May Love become

the ebb and flow

that hold my

world together.

Dear God,

please make me new.

May Your holy child
be born in me.
May every cell
of my being, dear God,
be now transformed
by grace.

Replace my fears
with love, dear God.
May Your power
emerge from the depths
of my heart.

Cast out my pain,

and grant me peace

on this most holy day.

Bless me, dear Lord,

and bless the world.

Amen

hepherds saw
a star in the sky.
Its light would become
a beacon of hope for
hearts throughout
the world.

Many of us, during the
dark nights of our soul,
look upward toward
a light that is not
of this world.

We are led to a child,
and that child is in us.
It is our divinity, our
tenderness, our true
authentic self. Fathered
by God and mothered
by human kindness,
the child is born in
all our hearts.

Let us all say:

yes, this holy child

shall find a home

on earth. This child

is gentler than the

gentlest snow,

and more powerful than
the most powerful king.
This child is one
with God. This child is
love incarnate. This child
is who we really are.

Dear God,
May the weariness
and darkness of my life
be cast out forever this
Christmas Day.
Dear God,
Please bless my life.

For I have seen

a holy star;

and it has lit my

inner skies.

May something new

be born in me —

A more loving self,

A more gentle self,

A more forgiving self,

A more peaceful self.
May the world
around me
thus be blessed.
May Christmas be
true for me this year,
and true for all the world.

Amen

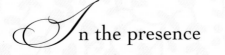

In the presence
of our most tender selves,
all powers of the world
are humbled.
Kings bear gifts
for the holy child,
for there is no power
in the outer world
that can compare to the
power of God.

The world is changed,
as secular power
defers to the dictates of
love. Neither technology
nor science nor worldly
wealth can compare
to the powers of
forgiveness and grace.

Holiness is the
greatest power of all.
At this Christmas season,
may it transform our lives
within and without.

A PRAYER
OF GIVING

Dear God,

At this Christmas season,

please open my heart.

May I learn

to be a giver,

not a taker,

For only thus

can I feel blessed.

Make of me
an instrument of
Your peace,
that peace might
fill my world.
May Your abundant
mercy touch my life.
May my heart so give
and so receive as to
expand to touch the stars.

May I so learn
to live with love,
that I might know of
heavenly bliss
while still on earth.
May the miracle
of Christmas
be a miracle in my heart.

Amen

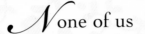one of us

is alone on earth.

We are all God's children.

We are all one family.

The people we know best,

whom we are born among

and live among, are the

source and often the

sustenance of our

relationships with the

larger world.

Healing and
strengthening our
family relationships,
and learning to foster
the joy of family,
is truly holy work.

Families and friends
form the emotional
structure of our lives.
The traditions of
Christmas tie our hearts
together, that we may
learn to live in peace with
those we know and love.

Christmas traditions dictate, with the power of the ages, that we be together with those we love. That we gift each other. That we seek to forgive what is unforgiven.

At Christmas,

we return to our families

and friends.

We call, we write,

we spend the day,

we remember.

As we learn to love
our families and friends
more deeply,
we more deeply learn
to love the world.

A PRAYER FOR
THE FAMILY

Dear God,

Please bless my family.

May Your angels come

upon us all,

and heal the places where

our hearts or ties

are hurt in any way.

May my mother,

my father,

my sister, my brother,

my mate, my children,

be blessed and sustained

wherever they are.

Help us to forgive

each other, for whatever

our trespasses.

Dear God,

Uplift this family.

Heal us all,

Make new our hearts,

Make strong the bonds

among us.

*May we reflect
Your light and
extend Your love.
May all who know us
be blessed thereby.*

Amen

Every day
can be like Christmas,
in its love and its peace,
if our hearts open up
and make room for love.

The holy child

is waiting to be born

in every instant,

not just once a year.

Not just one person,
but all humanity, is
yearning for the peace
of God. Not just one
family, but all the world,
is hoping for harmony
and forgiveness
and love.

Our greatest gift
to God, this holy
Christmas season, is to
commit ourselves to live
lives of peace.

Through God's help,
we can transform our
lives, and through
God's miracles,
we can transform
the world.

✦ A PRAYER ✦
FOR PEACE

Dear God,

May a great peace

come over me,

and over

all the world.

May forgiveness

come upon us

and make new all

living things.

May all wounds

be healed.

At Christmas,

this most holy season,

may peace prevail

in all our hearts.

May only love remain.

May every nation

live in peace,

and all humanity

become as one.

May the earth repair,

and her bountiful
harvests expand.
May Christmas
be a blessing
on us all.

Please grace us
with Your miracles
that we may be renewed.
Thank You, dear God,
God of light,
God of hope,
God of love.

Amen

Marianne Williamson is an internationally acclaimed author and lecturer. *A Return to Love, A Woman's Worth,* and *Illuminata* were #1 *New York Times* bestsellers. Her most recent book is *Enchanted Love: The Mystical Power of Intimate Relationships.*

A native of Houston, Ms. Williamson is now the Spiritual Leader of the Church of Today, the Unity Church in Warren, Michigan (Detroit metro area). She is a co-founder of the Global Renaissance Alliance.